GIANNINI LIBRARY

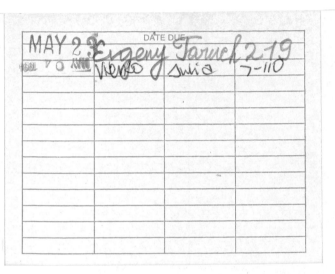

DATE DUE

AUSTRIA

Keith Lye

Franklin Watts

London   New York   Sydney   Toronto

Facts about Austria

Area:
83,849 sq. km.
(32,374 sq. miles)

Population:
7,555,000

Capital:
Vienna

Largest cities:
Vienna (1,502,000)
Graz (200,000)
Salzburg (139,000)
Innsbruck (117,000)

Official language:
German

Religion:
Christianity

Main exports:
Iron and steel, machinery,
timber and wood products,
chemicals, textiles

Currency:
Schilling

Franklin Watts
12a Golden Square
London W1

Franklin Watts Inc.
387 Park Avenue South
New York, N.Y. 10016

ISBN: UK Edition 0 86313 536 6
ISBN: US Edition 0 531 10365 X
Library of Congress Catalog Card No:
86–51548

© Franklin Watts Limited 1987

Typeset by Ace Filmsetting Ltd
Frome, Somerset
Printed in Hong Kong

Maps: Simon Roulstone
Design: Edward Kinsey
Stamps: Stanley Gibbons Limited
Photographs: Austrian National Tourist
Office 3, 7, 11, 15, 16; Chris Fairclough
12; ZEFA 4, 5, 6, 10, 13, 14, 17, 19, 20,
21, 22, 25, 28, 30, 31; J. Allan Cash 12,
18, 23, 24, 26, 27, 29
Front Cover: Zefa
Back Cover: Austrian National Tourist
Office

Austria is a small, mountainous
country in central Europe. It has no
coastline. Beautiful mountain ranges,
called the Alps, cover about seven
tenths of Austria. These mountains
run from Austria into Switzerland,
Italy, West Germany and France.

3

Austria's highest peak is called
Gross Glockner. It is 3,797 m
(12,547 ft) high in the Alps. Near it
is the Pasterzen Glacier. Glaciers are
bodies of ice made of compacted
snow. They slowly slide downhill.

4

The Danube is Austria's most important river. It starts in West Germany and flows across northern Austria on its way to the Black Sea. It is a busy waterway. Boats carry goods from Austria to nearby countries.

The northeastern part of Austria contains lowlands. These lowlands have most of the country's farmland. The picture shows a farming region bordering the Neusiedler Lake. This is Austria's largest lake.

The Neusiedler Lake is shallow and contains salty water. Eastern Austria has cold winters, but summers are warm and sunny. The mountains are much colder. Many are snowcapped throughout the year.

The picture shows some stamps
and money used in Austria. The
main unit of currency is the Schilling,
which contains 100 Groschen.

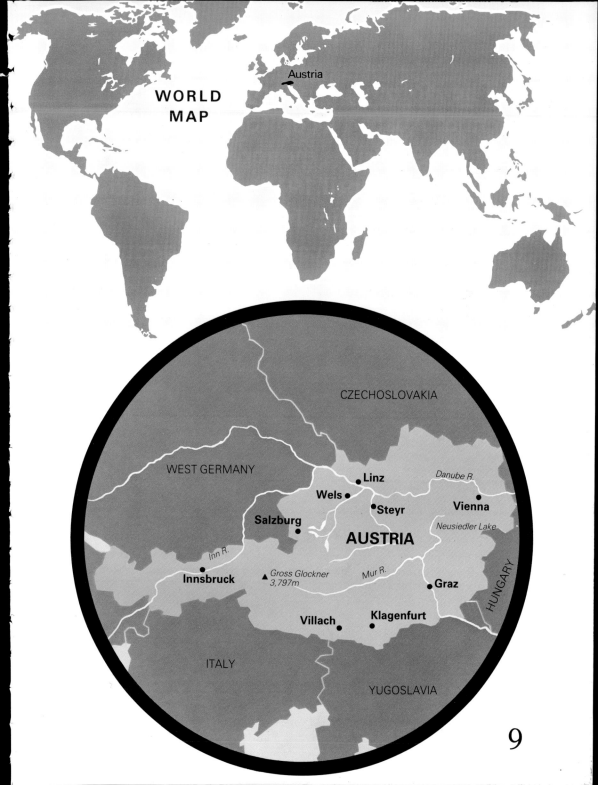

WORLD
MAP

Austria

CZECHOSLOVAKIA

WEST GERMANY

Danube R.

Linz

Wels

Steyr

Vienna

Salzburg

AUSTRIA

Neusiedler Lake

Inn R.

▲ Gross Glockner
3,797m

Mur R.

Innsbruck

Graz

HUNGARY

Villach

Klagenfurt

ITALY

YUGOSLAVIA

9

The Hofburg is a large palace in Vienna, Austria's capital. It was the home of Austria's monarchs from the 13th century until 1918, when Austria became a republic. It is now the official home of Austria's President.

The Hofburg contains the Spanish Riding School. Here, skilled riders perform on carefully trained, white Lipizzaner horses. Their displays recall the glories of the past, when Vienna was capital of a large empire.

Schönbrunn Palace in Vienna was
the summer home of Austria's
monarchs. The picture shows the
room where the emperor met visitors.
Austria's empire collapsed in 1918,
when Austria and its ally Germany
were defeated in World War I.

In 1945, after World War II, American, British, French and Russian troops occupied Austria. They withdrew in 1955. Austria is now a neutral federal republic. Its parliament in Vienna contains two houses, a Federal Council and a National Council.

Vienna is called Wien in German, Austria's official language. This great city has palaces, churches, museums and a zoo. One park, called the Prater, contains an amusement area with a huge Ferris wheel.

Graz, Austria's second largest city after Vienna, is in the southeast. The Old Town of Graz contains many beautiful buildings. About 56 out of every 100 people in Austria live in cities or towns.

Salzburg is Austria's third largest city. It stands on the Salzach River in the mountainous northwest. The city has a fine castle and cathedral. It is known for its yearly festival of music by Wolfgang Amadeus Mozart.

Innsbruck, Austria's fourth largest
city, is a resort in western Austria.
It stands in the valley of the Inn
River in the Alps. It was the site of
the Winter Olympics in 1964 and
again in 1976.

Austria is so mountainous that less than a fifth of the land can be used for farming. Hay is produced in the mountains to feed cattle in winter. The leading crops in Austria are barley, potatoes and wheat.

Livestock and dairy farming are major sources of income for farmers. Many farm animals spend the summer on mountain pastures and the winter in sheltered valleys. Farming employs 9 out of every 100 Austrian workers.

Forests cover about two fifths of
the land. Timber is one of Austria's
leading natural resources. Other
resources include coal and some
minerals. But most deposits are small.
Austria has to import many materials
for its factories.

Austria has many rivers. Dams have been built across many of them, creating lakes. The water is used to produce electricity in hydroelectric power stations. These stations account for more than seven tenths of the country's electricity supply.

Manufacturing and mining employ 41 out of every 100 Austrian workers. Many factories produce metals, such as steel, and metal products, such as cars and machinery. The main industrial city is Vienna. But this factory is in Steyr.

Craft industries are also important in Austria. Skilled people work in small factories, making such things as handbags, needlework, porcelain and wood carvings. Because of its many industries, Austria is a prosperous country.

Education for many children starts in a kindergarten. All children between 6 and 15 must attend school. Some schools are private, but most of them are run by the government and do not charge fees.

24

Austria has music schools which attract students from all over the world. Many children sing in choirs. The well known Vienna Boys' Choir sings every Sunday from September to June in a church in Vienna's Hofburg.

28587

Most city people live in apartments, but many country people live in one-family wooden homes. Austrians enjoy good food. The Austrian dish, Wiener schnitzel (thin pieces of breaded veal), is world famous.

At weekends and during vacations, Austrians take part in outdoor activities, including swimming, boating, fishing, water skiing and mountain climbing. This lake is at St. Wolfgang, a resort east of Salzburg.

The composer Wolfgang Amadeus
Mozart was born in this house in
Salzburg in 1756. It is now a museum.
Other famous Austrian composers
include Joseph Haydn, Franz
Schubert, Johann Strauss and
Gustav Mahler.

Salzburg's annual Mozart festival in July and August attracts many tourists. But music is performed throughout the year in Salzburg at indoor and outdoor concerts. Some bands play in the streets, squares and parks.

Winter sports include skiing, skating, tobogganing and ice hockey. Austria has many winter resorts, with excellent hotels and sports facilities. More than 15 million tourists visited Austria every year in the mid-1980s.

Austrians love festivals. Carnival, or Fasching, celebrations are held between January and Shrove Tuesday (the day before the start of Lent). Events during Fasching include processions with people in fancy dress and traditional dancing in folk costumes.

Index